MAS OYAMA'S

Essential

KARATE

MAS OYAMA'S
Essential
KARATE

By
MAS OYAMA

Sterling Publishing Co., Inc. · New York

Translated by Tomoko Murakami and Jeffrey Cousminer
Illustrations by Toshiaki Morishita
Photographs by Kodansha Ltd.

Fourteenth Printing, 1986

English translation copyright © 1978 by Sterling Publishing Co., Inc.
Two Park Avenue, New York, N.Y. 10016
Originally published in Japan © 1975 by Kodansha Ltd., Tokyo.
Distributed in Australia by Capricorn Book Co. Pty. Ltd.
Unit 5C1 Lincoln St., Lane Cove, N.S.W. 2066
Distributed in the United Kingdom by Blandford Press
Link House, West Street, Poole, Dorset BH15 1LL, England
Manufactured in the United States of America
All rights reserved
Library of Congress Catalog Card No.: 77–79509
Sterling ISBN 0–8069-4120-0 Trade
4121-9 Library

Contents

第一章
空手の沿革

Mas Oyama instructing a prince of the Jordanian royal family in the fine points of karate.

Foreword

Karate is currently enjoying wide popularity the world over. We encounter it frequently in books, films, and on television. There are few people who have not seen a demonstration of brick or wood breaking or a single bare-handed man defeat a host of armed opponents.

But karate is much more than this. It was developed over a thousand years ago, not only as a form of unarmed combat, but as a way to discipline the body in order to improve the spirit. In this way, a unity of body and spirit could be achieved.

If this sounds too abstract, perhaps we can use terms that are easier to deal with. Besides conditioning the body and improving speed, strength, and co-ordination, karate increases one's alertness and self-awareness. It also teaches confidence—not cockiness or brashness—but a deep confidence in one's abilities to deal with the world around him. And with confidence comes calmness and a sense of inner peace.

This is the true karate, the karate that one can practice years after he can no longer break bricks. But everything must have a beginning and great things cannot be accomplished in a handful of days. In karate, the beginning is the physical forms—the punches, kicks, and blocks that we have all seen. These are the techniques that enable an adept kareteka to perform the seemingly impossible feats that he does.

Not everyone who studies karate achieves success, but if you are able to master the techniques described in this book, you could be one of them. Work with patience and perseverance and you are sure to find some measure of satisfaction. You must also work with caution, always bearing in mind that karate is a combat form and enables one to deliver a blow of devastating power. Techniques applied improperly or with insufficient care could cause injury to you or others.

May your pursuit of karate be a rewarding one.

1. Fundamentals of Karate

第二章
空手の基礎

THE HAND AND ARM AS WEAPONS

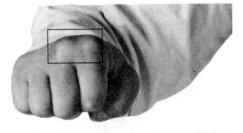

1. Seiken (normal fist)

This is the strongest and the most effective of the fist positions. *Seiken* is used when performing *Jodan-tsuki* (upper body thrust), a common position for attacking the face and the jaw; *Chudan-tsuki* (middle body thrust), the attack position for the chest and the stomach; and *Gedan-tsuki* (lower body thrust), for attacking the lower abdomen and groin. This fist can be used in defense as well as in attack.

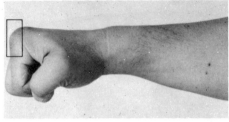

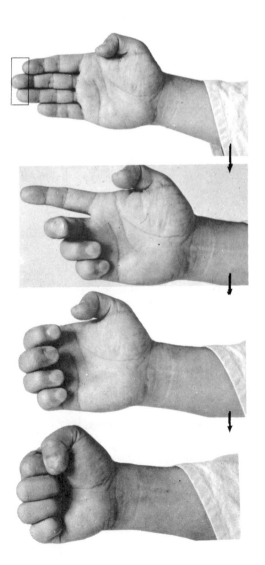

As shown in the first four photos, starting with the little finger, bend all four fingers so that their tips are digging tightly into the hand as close to their bases as possible. Bend the thumb over the second joints of the first two fingers to further tighten the fist.

When thrusting with the *Seiken,* you should strike the object directly with the knuckles of the first two fingers. In this position, if you strike an object with any of the other finger joints, you will most probably injure your hand. A punch with the fist in the *Seiken* position should be thrust straight out from the shoulder.

In the correct starting position, you should hold the fist with the palm facing up, touching your side on a level with your chest. Then, simultaneously, as you thrust forward, turn the fist inward so that at the point of attack the object will be struck by the knuckles of the first two fingers (in the final position, the palm should now be facing down). It is of utmost importance that at this point the arm and the back of the hand are held rigidly in a straight line, and that the object is being struck foremost by the knuckles of the first two fingers.

For beginners, the *Seiken* position is recommended for practice-sparring in order to avoid serious injuries while at the same time expressing great power.

A. *Seiken-chudan-tsuki* (middle body thrust with normal fist)

Starting with the fist in the normal position (the fist is held with the palm up, against the side and on a level with the chest), thrust forward in a straight line. At the point of striking the target, all the forward momentum should be transferred into the fist which is now held with the palm down. If there is any bend in the arm at this point, the transfer of power to the fist is inefficient. Further, it is probable that a wrist injury will result. It is obvious therefore, that you must time your punch so that it strikes the target a fraction of a second before the arm has reached its full extension in order for all its power to be spent on the target.

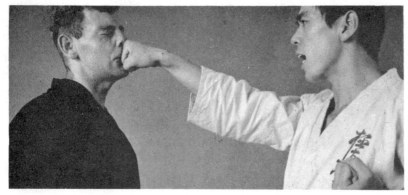

B. *Seiken-jodan-tsuki* (upper body thrust using normal fist)

The procedure for this is basically the same as that for *Seiken-chudan-tsuki;* however, you aim your punch at the facial area.

C. *Seiken-mawashi-uchi* (turning or roundhouse punch with normal fist)

Again, start with the fist in the normal position, but this time twist your body so that your fist is hidden from the opponent. Swing the striking arm outwards from the side in a large half-circle motion and strike the opponent on the side of the head or behind the ear. The twisting of the hips and the snapping back of the other arm is essential for maximum power to be generated in the striking fist. This punch is most useful against a taller attacker.

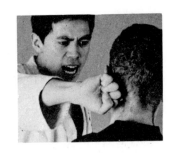

D. *Seiken-ago-uchi* (strike to the jaw with the normal fist)

For this punch, the striking hand is held at shoulder level and close to the body and the wrist is partially turned forward (unlike the previous techniques which have all begun with the hand in the basic position). The power for this punch is created by the sharp pulling back of the other arm simultaneous with the forward thrust. Unlike the previously described punches, this one should be pulled back immediately after striking the object.

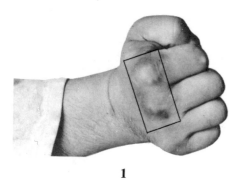

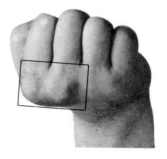

1

2

2. Uraken (back fist)

There are two basic methods for using this fist. In the first, the fist is clenched in the same way as it is in the *Seiken* position. However, in the *Uraken* position the object is struck by the back of the knuckles rather than the front (1). With this method, the spring action of the wrist facilitates the striking of an opponent who is either very close or at your side.

In the second method (2), the fist is held in the normal position for *Seiken*. The difference is in the thrust, for in this position the punch is delivered with the fist palm up. At the moment of impact, there should be a slight twist in the wrist to maximize this punch's effectiveness.

A. *Uraken-shomen-uchi* (back fist frontal punch)

In this position, the striking fist is held close to the body at about shoulder height, with the back of the hand facing the opponent. The fist is then thrust forward to strike the opponent's face. The actual striking can either be from directly in front or from slightly above, depending upon the degree of bending in the wrist.

B. *Uraken-sayu-uchi* (back fist one-two punch)

Here, the elbows and fists are held at chest height with the back of the hands facing the opponent. Then, using the elbows as pivots, thrust forward and strike with each fist in sequence. These punches are intended mainly for the face, and each should be pulled back immediately after hitting its mark (this will allow for greater speed). Maximum power will be created by the effective twisting of the hips as well as a pushing off from the opponent as each punch is thrown.

C. *Uraken-hizo-uchi* (back fist punch to the spleen)

In the starting position, the fists are held at navel level, one in front of the other. Then, using the elbows as pivots, thrust the fist to the opponent's side (either to the left or right, as needed). The primary target is the gut area.

 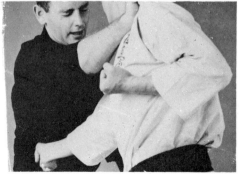

17

D. *Uraken-shita-tsuki* (back fist lower punch)

This punch is the exact opposite of the *Seiken-chudan-tsuki* in that although the primary positioning and forward thrust are the same, you strike with the fist palm up. It is particularly useful when you are grabbed suddenly by an opponent. Assume a low straddle stance as shown.

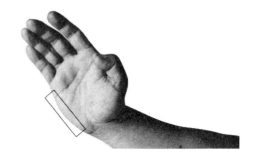

3. Tegatana (handsword)

In the handsword (or knifehand) the hand is open. The thumb is bent and held tightly against the edge of the hand. The four fingers are tensed, naturally curved and slightly apart. The outer edge of the hand is primarily used for striking.

A. *Tegatana-sakotsu-uchi* (handsword collarbone chop)

Hold the striking hand with the palm facing in, on a level with the ear, and swiftly bring the hand forward and down in an arc-like motion in order to hit the opponent's collarbone. Note that the other hand is also held in the *Tegatana* position in preparation for the next blow.

The collarbone is rather weak and a blow to it will cause difficulty in breathing and restriction of arm movement.

B. *Tegatana-sakotsu-uchikomi* (handsword collarbone strike)

Hold the hand at shoulder height and thrust forward to strike the opponent's collarbone. This differs from the previous technique in that there is more follow-through after the strike.

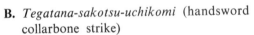

C. *Tegatana-ganmen-uchi* (handsword face chop)

Hold the striking hand as in A (*Tegatana-sakotsu-uchi*). Then bring the hand swiftly down across the face, ear, or neck of an opponent. At the moment of contact, the elbow should be slightly bent.

D. *Tegatana-naka-uchi* (handsword cross-body chop)

Hold the striking hand across your chest at the level of the opposite ear. Then bring the hand diagonally forward across your body in a straight line. The major targets are an opponent's face, neck, throat, and arms.

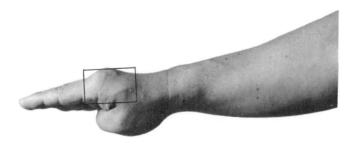

4. Segatana (reverse handsword)

In this position, the thumb is tucked into the palm and it is the inner edge of the hand that is used to strike. *Segatana* may be used from above or from the side; however, strikes thrown in this manner are weaker than those of *Tegatana,* and therefore it is rarely used.

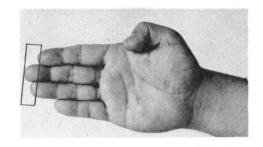

5. Nukite (piercing hand)

In this position, the hand is held in the same manner as in *Tegatana* except that the fingers are not separated. It is important that the fingers never be bent backwards, as serious injuries to the hand can result. The major targets are an opponent's stomach and throat.

A blow to the solar plexus with *Nukite* will render an opponent unconscious. Another common attack point is the lower rib cage (photo A). For the greatest effect, you should aim the blow between two ribs. An expert can nearly penetrate the body with this technique.

An attack to the throat will possibly cause lethal damage as this area is very soft and vulnerable (photo B).

A
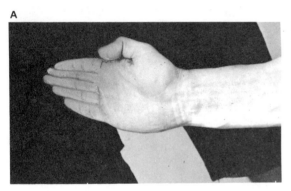

B
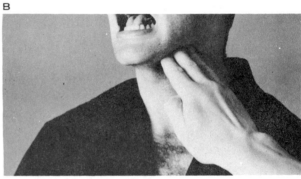

6. Variation of nukite

In this variation, the fingers are bent slightly inwards at the first knuckles. This is used when attacking with a roundhouse blow rather than a straight thrust. It allows for greater power and lessens the danger of a hand injury.

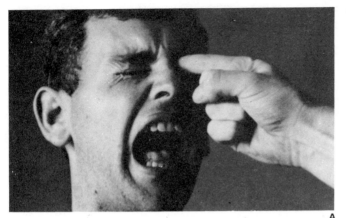

A

7. Ippon-nukite (one-finger piercing hand)

Here, the index finger (forefinger) is extended forward while the other fingers are bent into the palm, and the thumb bends tightly against the side of the middle finger. You thrust with this technique either with the back of the hand facing to the side or facing up. It is used to attack the eye (shown in photo A), below the nose, the throat, or the lower rib area. For best effect, the index finger should be bent very slightly inwards.

B
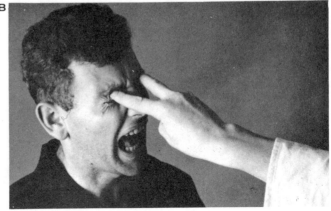

8. Nihon-nukite (two-finger piercing hand)

Here, the index and middle fingers are extended forward, while the other two fingers are bent with the thumb touching the ring finger.

Photo B illustrates the correct method for striking an opponent's eyes.

9. Keiko (chicken beak fist)

Bend the four fingers at the knuckles and bring the fingertips together. Then place the thumb underneath the tip of the middle finger. You strike an opponent from above or from the side using a quick snap of the wrist. The major target is the eye (photo A).

10. Oyayubi-ippon-ken (thumb fist)

This is the same as the *Seiken* position except that the thumb tip pushes against the area between

the first and second joints of the index finger, so that the first joint of the thumb sticks out. You strike an opponent with the thumb joint against the temple or below the ear lobe. CAUTION: This punch is extremely dangerous and could easily kill an opponent; therefore, use it with great care, and never make contact during practice.

Photo B illustrates the correct technique for striking the temple from the side.

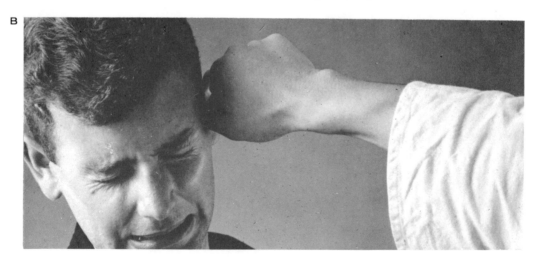

11. Hitosashiyubi-ippon-ken (forefinger fist)

This position is similar to the *Seiken* position, except that the second joint of the index finger should protrude and the thumb should press against the side of the nail of the index finger. You may attack either from above or from directly in front of an opponent. Targets are (A) the lower rib area, (B) beneath the nose, (C) the middle of the forehead, and (D) the throat.

A

B

C

D

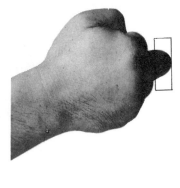

A

12. Nakayubi-ippon-ken (middle-finger fist)

This position is similar to *Hitosashiyubi-ippon-ken* except that it is the second joint of the middle finger which protrudes. The thumb pushes tightly against the area between the first and the second joint of the index finger. Attack procedure and targets are the same as for *Hitosashiyubi-ippon-ken*.

In addition to this position, there is also a combination of *Hitosashiyubi-ippon-ken* and *Nakayubi-ippon-ken* called *Nihon-ken* (two-finger fist), where the second joints of both the index and the middle finger protrude. Also, there is a technique known as *Ryutou-ken* (dragon's head fist), where the middle finger's second joint protrudes to form

the point of a triangle with the other fingers' second knuckles slightly protruding to form the triangle's sides.

Photo A illustrates striking beneath the lower lip using the middle-finger-fist technique.

13. Tettsui (iron hammer fist)

For this technique, the hand is put into the *Seiken* position. However, here it is the meaty outer edge of the hand that is used to strike the opponent. While this is not a sharp blow, it is a heavy and quite powerful weapon. You may attack from above to strike the head or shoulder of an opponent, or from the side in order to strike the temple, neck, or beneath the ear lobe.

Photo B illustrates this technique being applied from above to the back of an opponent's neck.

B

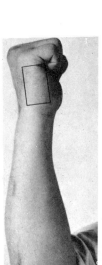
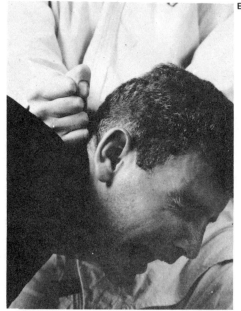

14. Shotei (palm heel thrust)

Here, you use the heel of the hand to strike an opponent. The blow is thrust forward powerfully in a pushing motion. Targets are the face and the jaw. This technique is also used against other areas in defense.

A. *Shotei* to the jaw from below.

B. *Shotei* to the spleen from the side.

C and **D.** The correct stance in preparation for performing the *Shotei-chudan* (middle body palm heel thrust).

E. *Shotei* to the stomach.

A

B

C

D

E

27

 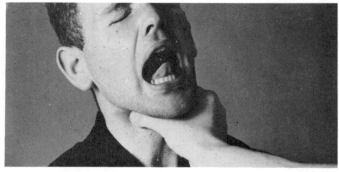

A

15. Toho (sword peak hand)

This is the wedge formed when the thumb is extended away from the rest of the hand. The target for this technique is the throat. Thrust forward and strike the opponent's throat strongly, as shown in photo A.

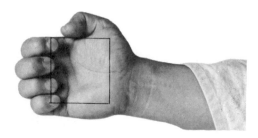

16. Heiken (flat fist)

In this position, the fingers are bent at the second joints as if to make a fist but the tips do not touch the palm. It is the first joints of the fingers and the palm that strike the object. Typical targets are the ear, the cheek, the throat, and the face. CAUTION: When applied to the ear, *Heiken* can rupture the eardrum.

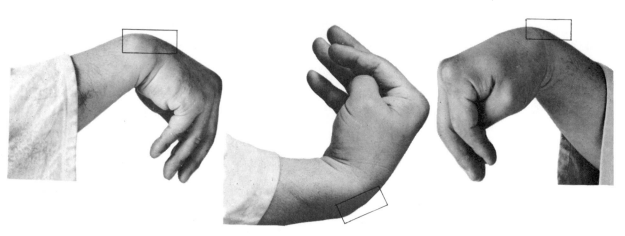

17. Koken (arc fist)

This position is formed by bending the wrist forward, and placing the thumb at the base of the middle finger. An opponent is struck with the exposed outer portion of the wrist. Targets include the spleen, face, and jaw. You can attack from above, below, or from either side of, an opponent. An advanced student can also use this as a defensive technique. Note that this wrist area is very sensitive, and when practicing, you should avoid striking hard objects.

A. *Koken* to the face from above.

B. *Koken* to below the ear lobe from above.

C. *Koken* to the jaw from below.

D. *Koken* to the spleen from the side.

E. *Koken* to the side of the neck with a diagonal blow.

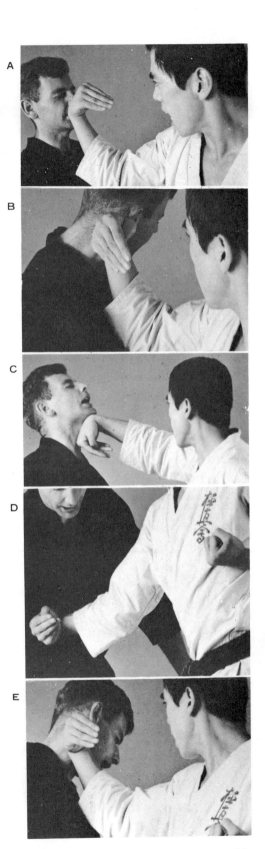

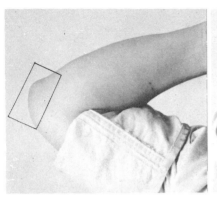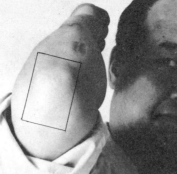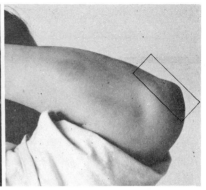

18. Hiji (elbow)

The elbow is considered to be the most devastating weapon in karate. It is a very hard bone and it is close to the shoulder, which generates much of the power for a blow. The elbow is used in four ways: it can strike down on an opponent, or it can strike up, or to the side, or to the back. It is used primarily when an opponent is in close proximity.

A. *Hiji* strike downwards on the back of an opponent's neck.

B. *Hiji* to the opponent's jaw from the side.

C. *Hiji* to the opponent's stomach from the side.

D. *Hiji* to the jaw from below.

A

B

C

D

19. Kote (forearm)

This is the part of the arm between the elbow and the wrist. It is most often used in defense as a block. The fist is held in either the *Seiken* or *Tegatana* positions. As shown in the photos, there are (1) forearm, (2) back forearm, and (3) front forearm. While *Kote* is mostly used for defense, the back forearm position may be used for striking an opponent's jaw.

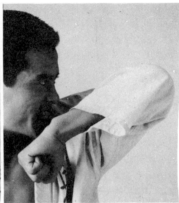

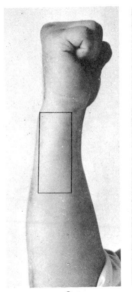

2   3

1

20. Additional upper body weapons

These are the head, the shoulder, and the teeth. The head may strike an object from any direction, but the primary target is an opponent's face. When practicing, do not use the head to strike hard objects. When using the shoulder, be sure to strike with the bony portion.

THE LEG AS A WEAPON

B B1

C C1

Due to the fact that the leg is normally used to support the body, it is more awkward to use as a weapon as compared to the arm. However, it is much stronger than the arm, and because of its superior length can be used to attack from a greater distance. It is generally accepted that the leg can express three times as much power as the arm.

A beginner must expect to lose his balance when first learning leg techniques. The three keys to successful mastery are: maintaining the center of gravity by keeping the hips steady, performing the kicks at great speed, and returning the striking leg to the ground immediately after the attack.

When you have developed sufficient strength and flexibility with your legs, you have acquired the strongest weapons in an unarmed man's arsenal. In competition karate, 70 per cent of the winning blows are delivered by the leg.

1. Ashigatana (footsword)

This is the outer edge of the foot, as shown in the photo. It is used to attack the neck, jaw, spleen, hips, and joints.

A

D D1

A. *Yoko-geri* (side kick)

Note that in this correct form, each foot and one shoulder form the vertices of a triangle.

B and **C.** *Yoko-geri* (side kicks, front and side views)

First, you transfer your weight to the supporting leg, keeping the hips steady and the knees slightly bent. Then pull up the kicking foot to a position just in front of the knee of the supporting leg. Now, quickly strike out with your leg to the side and immediately return to the starting position.

D. *Kansetsu-geri* (kicks to the knee)

Remember that immediately after delivering a kick, you must return the leg to its starting position. This allows for a quick follow-up kick, and prevents an opponent from catching you off balance.

E. *Ashigatana-yoko-geri-jodan* (upper body side kick using the footsword technique)

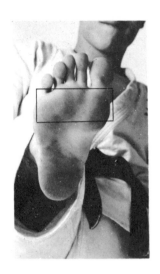

2. Naka-ashi (ball of the foot)

As shown in the photo at the left, this is the fleshy portion, or ball, of the foot just below the toes. In order to strike an opponent without injuring yourself, you must be sure to keep the toes bent back towards the shin. The targets are the temple, face, jaw, chest, and spleen.

A. *Mae-geri-age* (front upper kick)

B. *Chudan-mae-geri* (middle body front kick)

The first step is to bring the knee of the striking leg up above the navel. Then kick forward, striking the opponent's stomach or solar plexus. Be sure to keep the toes bent back to avoid injury. Note that to compensate for the forward kick, you must lean backwards approximately 25° in order to maintain balance. Also, your chest should be slightly concave and your chin tucked into your neck.

C. *Jodan-mae-geri* (upper body front kick)

This technique is basically the same as the previous ones; however, the primary targets are the jaw and face.

A

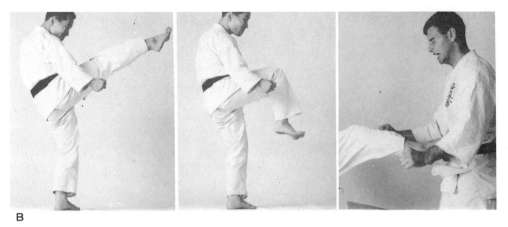

B

D. *Mawashi-geri* (roundhouse kick)

This kick starts in the same position as the above; however, the bent knee is brought to the side and the body is bent away from that

C

side. Then, using a large circular motion, extend your foot forward and strike the jaw, face or side. If the timing is correct, this kick can express a tremendous amount of power.

D

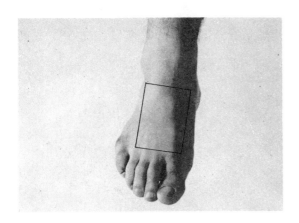 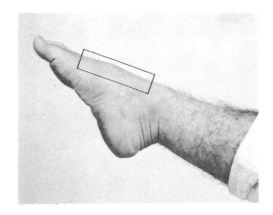

3. Seashi (instep)

As shown in the photos, this is the top of the foot just below the ankle. It is used to strike the groin, side, neck, and ribs. The toes are stretched straight forward.

A. *Mawashi-seashi-geri* (roundhouse kick with the instep)

This technique is basically the same as the turning kick described above, except that an opponent is struck with the instep rather than the ball. The chief target is the neck.

A

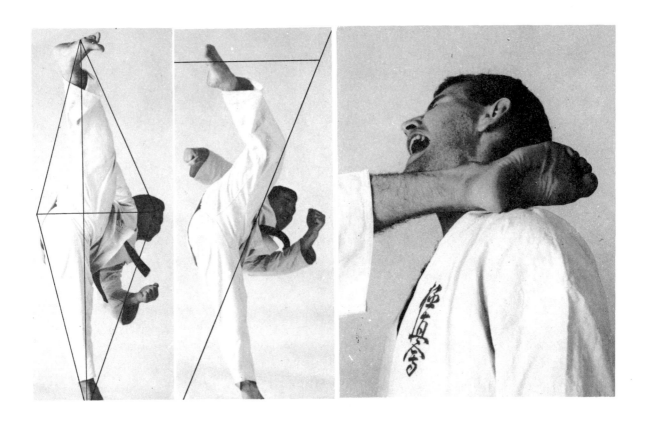

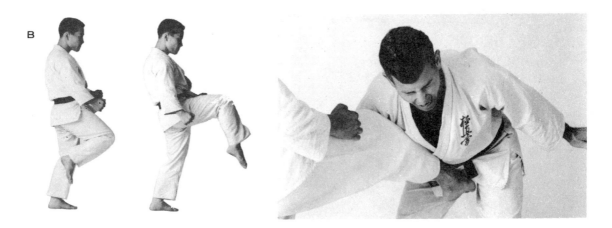

B. *Kinteki-seashi-geri* (testicles kick with the instep)
Bring the knee up and strike forward hitting the opponent's testicles with the instep. CAUTION: This target is the most vulnerable part of the male anatomy, so during practice you should never actually strike a sparring partner. *Kinteki-seashi-geri* is an excellent kick for a woman to use against a real attacker.

4. Soko-ashi (arch)

The arch is usually used for blocking an opponent's attack. It is always better to block a punch with a shock-absorber-like soft area such as the arch, rather than a hard area. This technique is also used to attack an opponent's side or arm with a sweeping sideways motion. (Photos below show front and side views of the *Soko-ashi* defense.)

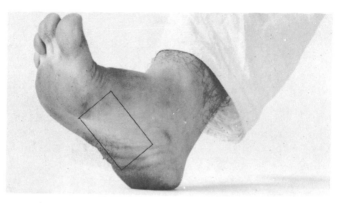

5. Kakato (heel)

The heel is the pivotal point for turning the body. It is also an effective weapon. There are two ways in which it can be used offensively:

A. *Kakato-geri* (heel kick)

This technique is used when the opponent is already on the ground. You bring the leg up, keeping it straight with the toes stretched back. Then bring the heel forcefully down against the opponent's head, face, or stomach. This is a very powerful and dangerous kick as all the body weight is concentrated in the heel.

B. *Ushiro-geri* (rear kick)

This form of attack is used for striking an opponent who is behind you. As illustrated, the correct technique is to drive your momentum backwards and your heel into the stomach of an opponent.

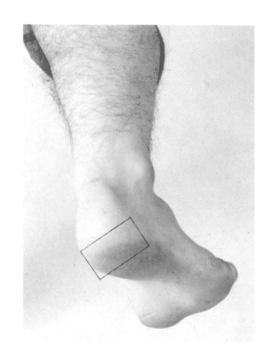

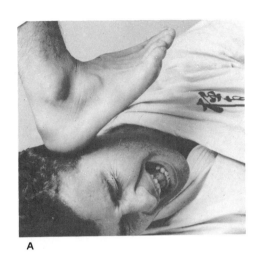

A

B

A. Front and side views of the knee kick using either leg.

6. Hiza-geri (knee kick)

The knee is as hard and powerful as the elbow, and also is most effective when fighting in close. The targets are the testicles, stomach, and thighs.

Another offensive technique is to grasp an opponent's hair and slam his face down against your knee. The knee and upper thigh can also be used defensively to block kicks from an opponent.

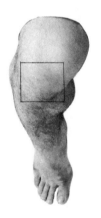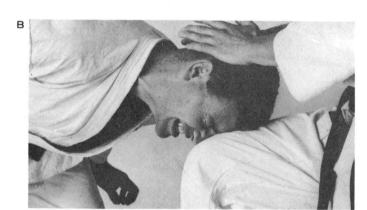

B. Technique of forcing an opponent's face onto your knee.

C. The correct procedure for using the knee kick to attack an opponent's thigh.

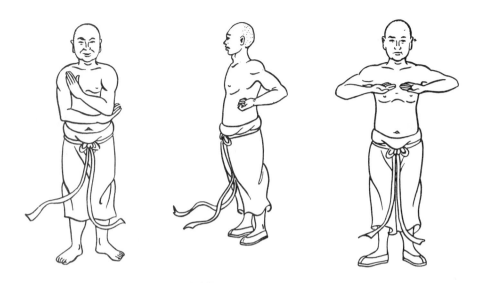

PRELIMINARY EXERCISES

To practice karate effectively and safely, you must first condition your body. These basic exercises should be performed often and repeatedly in order to build up strength and flexibility (and reduce the chances of injuries).

1

2

3

1. Wrist exercises

Start by standing with your legs slightly apart. Then bring your hands together, palms and fingers flat against one another (as shown in photos 1 through 6). Apply pressure and gradually bring your hands to chest level. Then start turning the fingers so that they point upwards, and at the same time raise your hands over your head. Make sure that the two hands always stay in contact with each other. Finally, return the hands to chest level as shown in photo 6.

4

5

6

2. Exercise for the Achilles tendon

Start by standing on your toes. In this position, bend your knees and drop your hips. Then, transfer the body weight to your heels, at the same time straightening your knees but still keeping the hips bent. This is one of the most important of all the preliminary exercises because any sudden strong tension on the Achilles tendon could rupture it. Therefore, it must be strengthened before you attempt any strenuous activities.

1

2

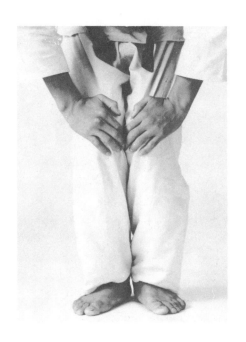

3. Knee exercise

This is primarily a flexibility exercise. Bend the knees deeply, hold them together with both hands, and rotate them to the left and then to the right. Strong, flexible knees are essential as they are the pivotal points for jumping and kicking.

4. Heel and ankle exercise

Lift one foot at a time and rotate the heel in a circular motion to the left and right. This will improve turning and elasticity.

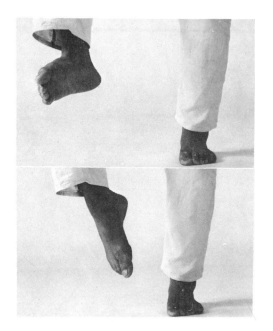

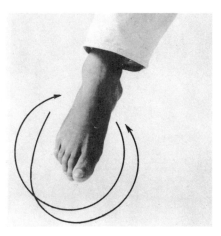

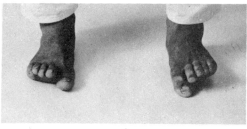

1   2

5. Toe exercise

Stand with the feet slightly spread and the hands grasping the belt. Lift the big toes as far off the ground as possible without lifting the other toes or the rest of the foot.

Then lift the other toes without lifting the big toes. This exercise will reduce the possibility of injuries to the toes resulting from improper kicking techniques, especially when performing *Naka-ashi* (ball-of-the-foot kick).

6. Hip exercise

Stand with the feet wide apart and hands clasped behind your head. Then bend forward without bending your knees, straighten up again, and bend backwards as far as possible. Practice this exercise until you are gradually able to do it with your legs close together.

2

7. Side exercise for roundhouse block

The roundhouse block (*Mawashi-uke*) is described on page 89. This exercise increases the flexibility and strength of the side muscles. From the starting position (1), pull the lower hand back against the side. Start bending to the side over that hand, and reach up and over the head with the other hand (2). Finally, thrust both hands towards the same side as if to ward off an attacker (3). Return to the starting position and repeat on the opposite side.

8. Back exercise for roundhouse block

Twist your body towards the back as far as possible (1). Then bend forward without bending the knees and touch the ground (2). Return to the standing position. Twist your body in the opposite direction, and repeat the exercise.

9. Push-ups

One variation of the push-up is to use only the fists to push off the ground. In another, your hands are flat against the ground. However, the best method is to use only the fingertips, starting with all five and gradually reducing the number as your strength increases. You should eventually be able to do push-ups with only one finger on each hand. Make sure that your hips neither protrude nor sag when doing this exercise.

10. Leg-stretching exercise

Sit with your legs spread apart as far as possible to either side. Grasp one knee with both hands and gradually pull until your chest is over that knee, being sure you keep the leg flat on the floor. Return to the starting position, place one hand on each ankle, and try to touch your chest to the floor. This exercise is good for stretching the calf and thigh muscles, which will improve the performance of any kicking technique.

11. Neck exercises

These exercises are important for developing a strong, flexible neck, which will protect the part of the spinal cord in this area. The exercises consist of rotating the neck around to the left and right, forward and backwards.

12. Back-stretching exercise

Start with your legs spread wide apart; then bend forward and support yourself on your fists and feet. Now, stretch your upper body as far forward as possible, and arch your back without touching your chest to the floor.

13. Knee-bend exercise

Bend your knees and lower your hips. Place your hands on the tops of the knees and straighten your legs while pushing against the knees. This exercise will aid extension of the legs when performing any of the kicking techniques.

14. Flexibility exercise for the legs

Start by spreading your legs wide apart. Bend one knee, keeping the other knee extended, and lower your body. Place one hand on each knee. Try to touch the calf of the extended leg to the floor by pressing down on the knee with your hand. Avoid leaning too far forward. Repeat the procedure with the other leg.

15. Finger exercise

Start with the fingertips together and gradually bring your hands together until the bases of the fingers (*not* the palms) are touching, by strongly pressing the fingers against each other (your knuckles should "crack").

16. Chest-to-feet exercise

Start in a seated position with the soles of the feet touching. Grasp your feet with both hands and bend the upper body forward until your chest is touching your feet.

17. Shotei-zuke (hip exercise)

This exercise begins in the *Musubi-tachi* stance (described on page 51). Bend your body forward at the waist, and touch the floor with your palms without bending your knees. Place the hands close to the feet and gradually move them until they are behind the feet, still flat on the floor with the fingers pointing back. Vary this exercise by spreading the legs wide apart and placing the right palm in front of the left leg. Repeat with the left hand and the right leg.

STANCES

Of primary importance to the successful performing of karate is learning the correct stances. The new student of karate must place himself in the position of a baby and learn to stand all over again. Like the baby's, your mind must be totally receptive to new experiences.

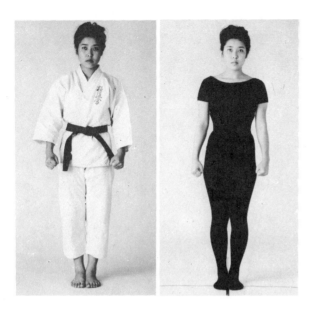

1. Heisoku-tachi (blocked foot stance)

In this stance, the feet are held tightly together with the spine and neck in a straight line. The arms should drop naturally to the sides and the fists should be clenched. In this, as in all stances, you must always face straight ahead and relax the inner self by blocking out all thoughts.

2. Musubi-tachi (open foot stance)

This stance is identical to *Heisoku-tachi* except that the heels are touching, and the toes are separated at a 60° angle. This stance is often used at the beginning of *Kumite* and *Kata*.

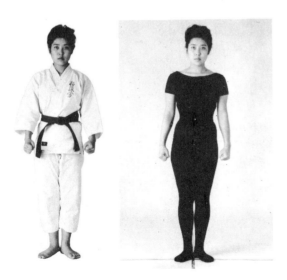

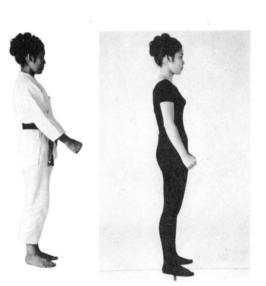

3. Heiko-tachi (parallel foot stance)

The feet are separated to shoulder width and the toes are pointed straight ahead. This is a common stance used for both attacking and defending.

4. Zenkutsu-tachi (forward stance)

In this position, one leg extends behind the body with the knee kept straight and the foot turned outwards. Lean the upper body forward slightly, and bend the front leg. The distance from left to right between the two legs should equal the width of the shoulders.

5. Kokutsu-tachi (back stance)

Extend one leg forward so that only the toes are touching the floor. The back leg is bent and the hips dropped. Two-thirds of the body weight is supported by the back leg. The front foot is pointed to the front and the back foot turned outwards. The legs are shoulder width apart. This stance is used in *Naka-uke* (page 65) and *Tsuki* (page 14).

6. Fudo-tachi (ready stance)

This stance is the same as *Heiko-tachi* except that the feet are both turned outwards. The shoulders should be naturally relaxed as this is a preparative stance for action to follow.

7. Shiko-tachi (Sumo stance)

This is a basic stance derived from Sumo wrestling. The legs are spread apart to twice the width of the shoulders, with the knees bent and the feet turned outwards. The hips are dropped and the spine is straight. The upper body should be supported by the hips. In this position (as well as the next one), the center of gravity is much lower than in most other stances. Therefore, you must have strong legs and hips for good balance. For obvious reasons, this is not a good stance for executing swift kicking techniques.

8. Kiba-tachi (horse stance)

This stance is the same as *Shiko-tachi* except that the feet are pointed forward and tension is placed on the inner parts of the feet. The position is similar to that of riding a horse.

9. Sansen-tachi (fighting stance)

This is a common practice stance. One foot is placed one step forward so that its heel is on the same horizontal line as the toes of the back foot. Both feet are turned in. The distance between the toes of each foot is shoulder width. The tension is placed along the inner edges of the feet, allowing for a very stable posture.

The photos below show how to convert from *Heiko-tachi* (see page 52) to *Sansen-tachi* by bringing one foot towards the other using a circular motion so that the feet briefly touch and then separate. The moving foot should end up one step in front and to the side of the stationary foot.

10. Tsuru-ashi-tachi (crane stance)

Here, the body is supported on one leg. The sole of the raised foot is placed against the inside of the knee, like a crane standing on one leg. In this stance, you should be ready to strike with *Yoko-geri* (side kick) and *Uraken* (back fist). This is a transitional stance between a period of defense and attack.

11. Naka-hachiji-tachi (inner figure 8 stance)

This is named for the resemblance of the position of the feet to the Japanese character for the numeral 8. The feet are shoulder width apart, with the toes turned in and the heels turned out. The tension should be placed along the inner edges of the feet, spine, and the sides.

12. Soto-hachiji-tachi (outer figure 8 stance)

This is similar to *Fudo-tachi* (ready stance) except that the feet are wider apart and therefore the stance is more stable.

13. Kake-ashi-tachi (hooked foot stance)

Like *Tsuru-ashi-tachi*, this is a transitional stance used to smooth out conversions from one movement to another. Starting from any stance, move one leg backwards and place it as if hooking it behind the knee of the other leg. Only the toes touch the ground—the back of the foot should be raised. This stance enables you to do one of two things—to either drop back one step or to prepare for executing a kick.

14. Futa-ashi-tachi (two-legged stance)

Stand with the feet one shoulder width apart. Place one foot just in front of the other with the toes pointing forward. The knees should be relaxed, making this a rather loose and versatile preparative stance.

15. Neko-ashi-tachi (cat stance)

This stance is very similar to *Kokutsu-tachi* except that the distance between the front and back feet is narrower. Ninety per cent of the body weight is supported by the back leg. Because the front leg is held very loosely, its great flexibility allows for very successful kicks. It is generally true that the narrower the stance, the faster the leg action.

16. Shumoku-tachi or Toboku-tachi (T-shaped stance)

Place one foot with the toes pointing straight forward. Place the second foot perpendicular to the first, making a 90° angle. The heels of both feet are touching, and the body faces directly forward.

UKE (DEFENSE)

You should never feel that defense means passivity and accept the rôle of the underdog; instead, confidently expect to win every fight. You can never improve without absolute belief in your own abilities.

A

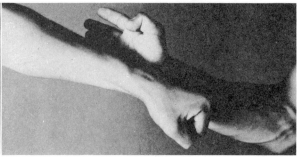

B

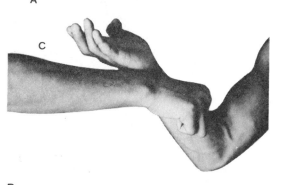

C

D

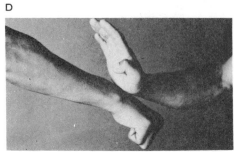

E

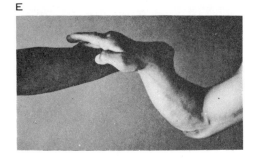

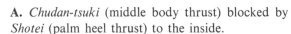

1. Defense against hand attacks

You must develop your defense techniques so that they become the first step in a counter-attack. Every block should be transformed into some sort of offensive weapon. With this in mind, you can understand the importance of thoroughly mastering the basic defense techniques.

A. *Chudan-tsuki* (middle body thrust) blocked by *Shotei* (palm heel thrust) to the inside.

B. The same defense except that the thrust is blocked to the outside.

C. A thrust blocked by *Tegatana* (handsword).

D. A punch blocked by *Shotei* (palm heel thrust) from above.

E. A punch blocked by *Tegatana-kake* (handsword hook). This block is the same as C except that the wrist is turned inwards. with the palm facing down.

F. A punch blocked to the outside with *Koken* (arc fist).

G. *Koken* from above.

H. *Koken* from below.

I. *Hirate-tsukami* (flat hand grasp)
Even though this is called a "grasp," it is actually

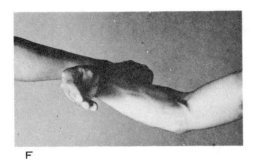

F

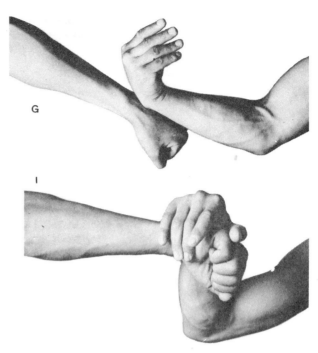

G

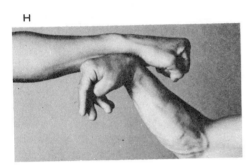

H

I

only a hooking block. As you can see in the photo, the thumb and the fingers do not close around the

opponent's fist but merely swat it away. This technique is used very often.

2. Defense against leg attacks

For defending against kicking attacks, you can use either your arms or legs. However, the arms are used to block more often because leg blocks are much slower, although timing can be greatly improved by constant practice.

A. *Mawashi-geri* (roundhouse kick) blocked by *Hidari-jodan-heiko-uke* (upper body parallel block using the left hand) to the right leg.

B. *Mawashi-geri* (roundhouse kick) blocked by *Jodan-heiko-soto-uke* (upper body parallel block to the inside) to the left leg using the left hand.

A

B

C. *Mae-geri* (front kick) blocked by *Gedan-barai* (lower body sweep).

D. *Mae-geri* (front kick) blocked by *Shotei-uke* (palm heel block).

E. *Mae-geri* (front kick) blocked by *Gedan-juji-uke* (lower body X-block).

F. *Mae-geri* (front kick) blocked by *Gedan-tegatana-juji-uke* (lower body handsword X-block).

G. *Mae-geri* (front kick) blocked by *Soko-ashi-naka-uke* (arch block to the outside).

H. *Mae-geri* (front kick) blocked by *Hiza-soto-uke* (knee block from the outside).

C

D

E

F

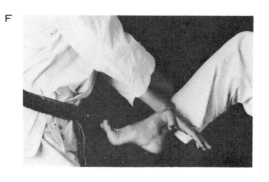

G

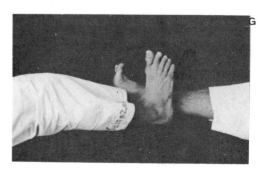

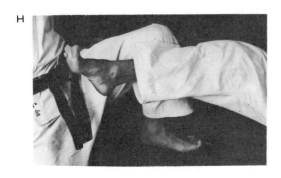

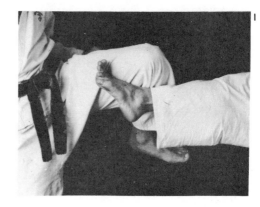

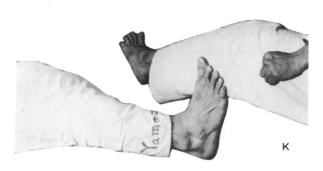

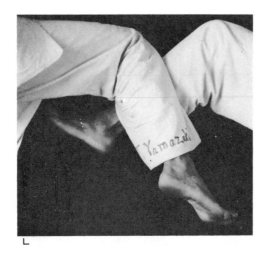

I. *Mae-geri* (front kick) blocked by *Hiza-naka-uke* (knee block to the outside).

J. *Mae-geri* (front kick) blocked by the shin from the inside.

K. *Mae-geri* (front kick) blocked by an arch block to the inside.

L. *Mae-geri* (front kick) blocked by the shin to the inside.

①

3. Applying blocking techniques

A. *Jodan-uke* (upper body block)

In the correct position for this technique (shown here), the blocking hand is held at a distance of two fists from the head, while the other hand is held at chest level.

(1) *Jodan-tsuki* (upper body thrust) blocked by *Jodan-uke* (upper body block).

(2) Various applications of *Jodan-uke*.

②

①　　②

B. *Soto-uke* (block from the outside)
(1) In the performance of this block, the blocking hand is rotated from a position next to the ear to a point in front of the eyes. The other hand remains at chest level.
(2) In this block, you should use the muscular area below the elbow when making actual contact. For the most effective block of a punch, always aim for the opponent's wrist (this is very important to remember).

C. *Naka-uke* (block from the inside)
(1) *Chudan-tsuki* (middle body thrust) blocked from the inside.
(2) When you anticipate a very powerful punch, support the blocking arm with your other arm.

①　　②

①   ②

D. *Tegatana-jodan-uke* (handsword upper body block)

(1) Side view of *Tegatana-jodan-uke* using the left arm.

(2) *Tegatana-jodan-uke* from the front.

(3) *Jodan-tsuki* (upper body thrust) blocked by *Tegatana-jodan-uke* to the outside.

E. *Shotei-uke* (palm heel block)

(1) *Shotei-sotogawa-uke* (palm heel block from the outside).

(2) *Shotei-shita-uke* (palm heel block from above).

(3) Side and front view of *Shotei-uke*.

F. *Tegatana-uke* (handsword block).
(1) *Tegatana-uke* with the left hand.
(2) *Migi-jodan-tsuki* (upper body thrust with the right hand) blocked by *Hidari-tegatana-soto-uke* (handsword block from the outside with the left hand).

(3) *Chudan-tsuki* (middle body thrust) blocked by *Tegatana-gedan-barai* (lower body sweep).
(4) Transition from *Tegatana-jodan-uke* (upper body handsword block) to *Kake-uke* (hook block).

G. *Koken-ue-uke* (arc fist block from below)
This technique is used more to deflect, rather than block, an opponent's punch.
(1) A right-hand punch blocked by *Koken* (arc fist) with the left hand.
(2) *Koken-ue-uke* as seen from the front and the side.

①   ②   ③   ①

H. *Koken-yoko-uke* (arc fist block to the side)
(1) Front and side views.
(2) A left middle body elbow attack blocked by *Koken-chudan-naka-uke* (arc fist middle body block to the outside).

(3) A right-hand middle body punch blocked by *Koken-chudan-naka-uke* (arc fist middle body block from the inside).

I. *Koken-oroshi-uke* (arc fist block from above)
(1) This technique resembles *Koken-oroshi-uchi* (arc fist attack from above).

(2) *Migi-chudan-tsuki* (middle body punch with the right hand) blocked by *Koken-oroshi-uke* with the left hand.

①   ②

J. *Segatana-uke* (reverse handsword block)
(1) *Chudan-tsuki* (middle body thrust) blocked by *Segatana-uke* from the outside.
(2) *Chudan-tsuki* blocked by *Hidari-segatana-uke* (reverse handsword block with the left hand). When an opponent's punch is very strong, you can strengthen your block by supporting the blocking arm with your other hand. This is a very powerful defense.

K. *Shotei-ue-uke* (palm heel block from below)
(1) Front view.
(2) *Migi-jodan-tsuki* (upper body thrust with the right hand) blocked by *Shotei-ue-uke* with the left hand.

L. *Gedan-barai* (lower body sweep)
(1) Front view.
(2) Side view.
(3) A middle body punch blocked by *Gedan-barai*.

(4) During practice, start in *Sansen-tachi* (fighting stance). An opponent's left-hand punch should be blocked by the right hand from the inside, and a right-hand punch should be blocked by the left hand, also from the inside.
(5) *Gedan-barai* (with the left hand) and *Migi-naka-uke* (right block from the inside) being performed (front and side views).

M. *Jodan-juji-uke* (upper body X-block)
(1) *Jodan-tsuki* (upper body thrust) blocked by *Juji-uke* (X-block).

(2) *Jodan-tsuki* blocked by *Tegatana-juji-uke* (X-block using the handsword technique).

①

②

2. Application of Fundamental Techniques

第三章　基本の応用

Karate is made up of four basic movements: forward, backwards, turning and jumping. However, you should avoid moving backwards whenever possible, and strive to keep the direction of attack forward, blocking as you go. Rather than retreating backwards under the assault of an opponent, turn to the side in order to throw him off balance, or block the attack and convert your block into an offensive weapon. You should enter every combat with the idea that there is no retreat; the momentum of battle should always be forward.

OI-TSUKI (LUNGE PUNCH)

This is a type of "shadow boxing" using karate techniques. You perform a series of from 3 to 5 attacks and blocks while moving forward, and conclude with a turn. Although you practice these moves alone, you must feel as though you were actually fighting a live opponent, and try to project a sense of tremendous power.

Turning

Even though it has been taught in all karate schools that basic techniques for attacking and blocking an opponent follow a straight-line progression, actually the more natural and effective technique is a circular movement. This should, therefore, be stressed during every practice session.

1. Chudan-oi-tsuki (middle body lunge punch)

Begin in *Fudo-tachi* (ready stance) (1), then move the right leg one step back and pull the right fist against the right side of the chest. The left arm is in *Hidari-gedan-barai* (left lower body sweep) position (2). From here, move the right leg one step forward and perform *Migi-chudan-seiken-tsuki* (right middle body thrust with normal fist) (3). Then repeat this procedure with the left leg and arm as you move another step forward (left middle body thrust with normal fist) (4).

2. Turn after Chudan-oi-tsuki (middle body lunge punch)

No matter how many times you perform *Chudan-oi-tsuki,* eventually you must turn around. At the moment that you have made the last blow with the right hand, move the rear (left) leg across to the right and pivot 180° on both feet at the same time, while performing *Hidari-gedan-barai* (left lower body sweep). This will exactly reverse your position. From here, continue *Chudan-oi-tsuki* and repeat the entire series back and forth several times.

3. Chudan-gyaku-oi-tsuki (middle body lunge punch from the reverse position)

This is the same as *Chudan-oi-tsuki* except that the right arm thrust coincides with the left leg forward step, and vice versa.

4. Jodan-oi-gyaku-tsuki (upper body lunge punch from the reverse position)

This technique is the same as *Chudan-gyaku-oi-tsuki,* except that the arm thrusts are directed towards the head of an opponent. The turning technique is the same as the one previously described.

5. Chudan-soto-uke (middle body block from the outside)

This is the same as *Chudan-oi-tsuki* except that instead of an offensive attack, you are performing a defensive block from the outside. When turning at the end of one forward sequence, you pull the left leg to the back and go into the left forward stance (*Hidari-zenkutsu-tachi*).

6. Chudan-gyaku-soto-uke (middle body block from the outside from the reverse position)

This defense is the same as *Chudan-soto-uke* except that the right arm block coincides with the forward step of the left leg, and vice versa.

7. Jodan-uke (upper body block)

This is a defensive technique for blocking blows from above. The basic procedure is the same as for those previously mentioned, except that the block is aimed higher.

8. Jodan-gyaku-uke (upper body block from the reverse position)

This is the same as *Jodan-uke* except that the right hand block is coincidental with the forward step of the left leg.

9. Zenkutsu-hiji-age-uchi (forward elbow upper thrust)

Starting from a forward stance, perform a lower body sweep, then put the right leg forward, and at the same time perform an elbow upper thrust with the right arm. Then continue on, moving to the other side.

10. Zenkutsu-gyaku-hiji-age-uchi (forward elbow upper thrust from the reverse position)

This is the same as *Zenkutsu-hiji-age-uchi* except that the right elbow thrust coincides with the forward step of the left leg, and vice versa.

11. Hiji-soto-uchi (elbow thrust from the outside)

This technique is very similar to *Zenkutsu-hiji-age-uchi* except that the thrust is performed to the front and side of an opponent's head in a sweeping motion. The leg and arm movements are the same as in 9.

12. Hiji-gyaku-soto-uchi (elbow thrust from the outside from the reverse position)

This is the same as *Hiji-soto-uchi* except that the right elbow outer thrust coincides with the forward step of the left leg, and vice versa.

76

13. Sansen-tsuki (fighting blow)

Starting from the *Sansen-tachi* (fighting stance), perform *Migi-chudan-tsuki* (right middle body thrust). Repeat with *Hidari-chudan-tsuki* (left middle body thrust).

14. Sansen-gyaku-tsuki (fighting blow from the reverse position)

This technique is the same as the previous one except that the right arm thrust coincides with the forward step of the left leg, and vice versa.

15. Turn after Sansen-tsuki (fighting blow)

Starting from the fighting stance with the right leg slightly in front (right fighting stance), pivot on the left leg 180° to the left and end up in the left fighting stance.

16. Tegatana-uke (handsword block)

From *Hidari-gedan-barai* (left lower body sweep position), step forward with the right leg; this is the back stance (*Kokutsu-tachi*). At the same time, bring the right hand forward in *Tegatana-uke*. Continue, alternating left and right.

18. Shotei-uke (palm heel block)

Stand in either the back stance or the cat stance, and perform a left lower body sweep (*Hidari-gedan-barai*). Then, put the right leg one step forward and perform a right palm heel block. Continue, alternating left to right.

17. Turn after Tegatana-uke (handsword block)

Starting from left *Tegatana-uke* (this is the position you should be in at the end of one complete series), turn to the right by pivoting 180° on both heels. At the same time, gradually reverse the position of the hands so that you end up in right *Tegatana-uke* position.

19. Shotei-gyaku-uke (palm heel block from the reverse position)

This is the same as *Shotei-uke* except that the right *Shotei-uke* coincides with the forward step of the left leg, and vice versa.

20. Segatana-uke (reverse hand-sword block)

This technique is the same as *Shotei-uke* except that a reverse handsword is performed instead of a palm heel block.

21. Koken-uke (arc fist block)

This is the same as *Shotei-uke* except that an arc fist block is performed. The blocking hand should be held at eye level. (Both 20 and 21 may be performed from the reverse position.)

22. Kaiten-jun-tsuki (turn and thrust)

Start by performing a lower-body sweep (*Hidari-gedan-barai*) with the left hand; then begin to step forward with the right leg while pivoting 90° on the left leg. At the end of the pivot, the right leg should be very close to the left leg, but still not touching the ground. From here, thrust forward both the right leg and arm. You should now be in a horse stance, one foot in a direct line with the other. Continue, alternating from left to right. Note that this technique is very fast; even though it looks like a long time is taken to perform a single pivot and thrust, actually this is almost instantaneous.

OI-GERI (LUNGE KICK)

1. Oi-mae-geri (front lunge kick)

Starting with a lower body sweep (*Hidari-gedan-barai*), with the arms held loosely, kick with the right leg to the opponent's chest. It is important when performing this to bring down the kicking leg very gently to avoid injury to the foot. Continue, alternating the kicks from the left leg to the right leg.

2. Oi-mae-geri-age (front lunge upper kick)

This technique is the same as *Oi-mae-geri* except that you aim the kick higher, towards an opponent's face and head.

3. Oi-yoko-geri-age (side lunge upper kick)

Starting from the horse stance (*Kiba-tachi*), pivot 180° on the left leg and perform a side kick with the right leg. Continue, alternating the legs from left to right. Make sure that you drop your kicking leg gently after kicking.

4. Oi-mawashi-geri (roundhouse lunge kick)

Start as in *Oi-mae-geri* (front lunge kick), move the right leg forward using a circular motion and strike an opponent's jaw with *Naka-ashi* (ball of the foot). Continue, alternating legs.

5. Oi-ashigatana (lunge foot-sword)

Starting from *Han-kiba-tachi* (half horse stance), pivot 180° on the left leg and perform a footsword kick to the side with the right leg. Continue, alternating legs.

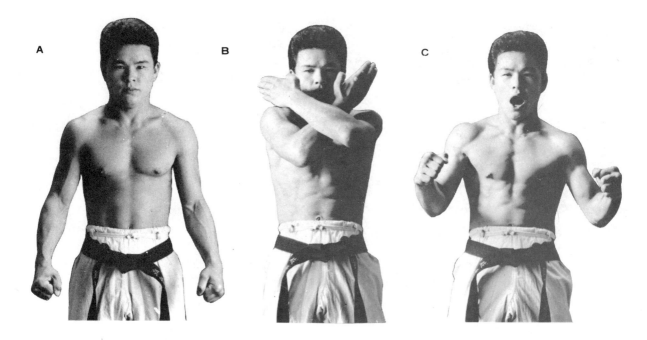

BREATHING

One of the most important aspects of karate is breathing correctly. The average person uses his lungs to only 60 per cent of their full capacity, and it is essential for the karateka (one who practices karate) to improve upon this. The part of the body that is particularly affected by breathing is the lower abdomen, which is 5 to 10 cm below the navel. The muscle found in this area must be very strong and taut in order to perform karate with the utmost effectiveness, and the correct breathing technique will improve the muscle tone of this area greatly. Of course, correct breathing will also improve the whole body, as well as the mind.

1. Ibuki

This series of breathing techniques is called *Ibuki* in karate, and should be practiced repeatedly on a daily basis. (The pictures at the bottom of the pages show side views of *Ibuki*.)

A–B: Stand with both hands clenched tightly, and inhale so quietly that no one will be able to hear you. As you inhale, gradually bring your arms up and cross them on either side of the head. Inhale slowly and fully, all the time trying to force the air down into the lower abdomen.

C–D: When you have inhaled to your fullest capacity, exhale noisily, trying to force the air out by using the lower abdomen. While exhaling, uncross your arms and clench your fists and gradually lower them to your sides. Towards the end of the exhalation, tense all the muscles in the body, especially in the abdomen.

E: The body at the completion of one breathing cycle.

D

E

2. Front breathing

A. Stretch both arms out to the front.

B. Turn both hands palm upwards.

C. Inhale deeply in a quiet manner as you gradually bring both hands back to your chest.

D. Lower the hands gradually.

E. Turn the hands palms down and begin to exhale quietly. Continue lowering the hands.

F. Completion of one breathing cycle.

In combat you must exhale silently so that your opponent will not know when you are out of breath—at the end of an exhalation the body is very vulnerable. For one thing, movements and reactions are slowed down, and for another, blows to the body at this time produce the greatest shock to the system. When there is air in the lower abdominal area, blows to the body do not produce so great a shock. For these reasons, you should exercise so that you can prolong the period of time that air remains in the lower abdomen.

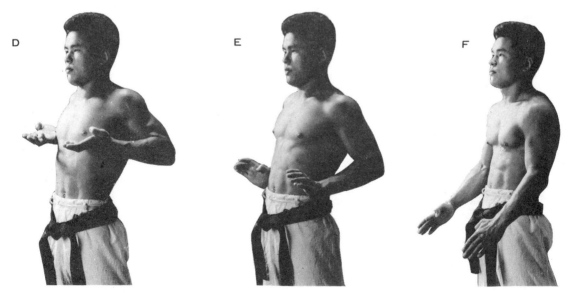

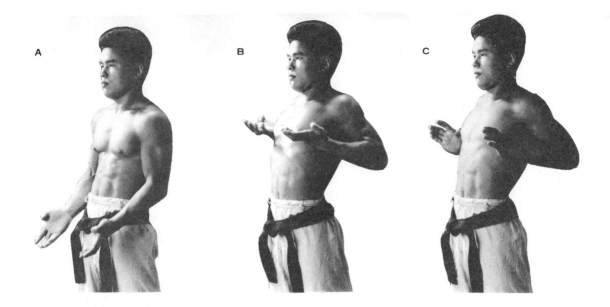

3. Back breathing

The repeated practice of this exercise is very important for the best performance in karate.

A. Stand with the arms bent slightly at the elbow and the hands held with the palms up.

B. Start to inhale, gradually bringing the hands up to shoulder level.

C. At the peak of inhalation, stop, and tense all the muscles, especially the elbows, legs, and middle fingers. Gradually turn the hands palm down.

D. Gradually lower the hands but keep the fingers tensed as if you were going to thrust them at an opponent.

E. Holding your breath, tense the lower abdomen, sides, and fingertips, and extend the hands forward.

F. From this position, relax and exhale, gradually lowering your arms to the position in A (palms should gradually be turned up).

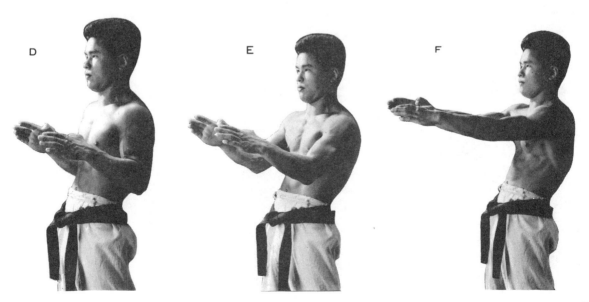

THE POINT AND CIRCLE

As was previously mentioned, although many schools of karate stress linear motion, actually the most effective techniques are those that utilize circular movements. It is interesting to note that the martial arts in India and China stress circular movements.

According to studies in kinetic energy, the greater the centrifugal force present the greater the distance the circumference of a circle is from a center. Therefore, the karateka should think of his hips as the center of a circle and perform his punches as though outlining the circumference of a large circle. This will make for much more powerful blows than punches thrown in a direct linear fashion.

The techniques in the photos here illustrate this concept of performing punches, blocks and sweeps in a circular or curvilinear motion.

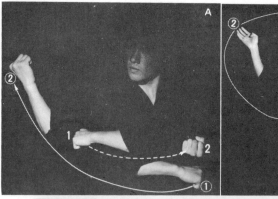

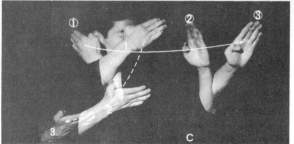

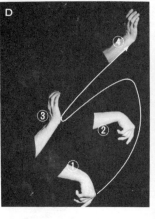

A. *Chudan-naka-uke* (middle body block from the inside)

B. *Enkei-shotei-shita-uke* (palm heel block from above in a circular motion)

C. *Tegatana-naka-uchi* (handsword cross body chop from the inside)

D. *Koken-shotei-uke* (arc fist-palm heel block)

E. *Jodan-uke* (upper body block)

F. *Jodan-seiken-tsuki* (upper body thrust using normal fist)

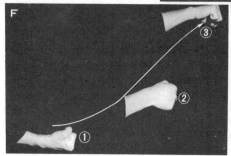

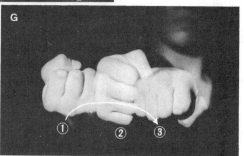

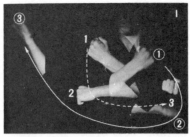

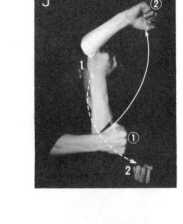

G. *Jodan-seiken-tsuki* (front view)

At the instant that the fist comes in contact with the object, it should be twisted as illustrated.

H. *Gedan-oroshi* (lower body drop punch)

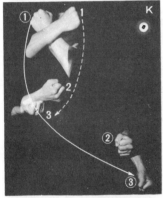

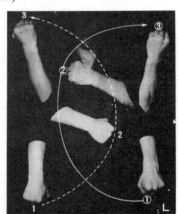

I. *Chudan-naka-uke* (middle body block from the inside)

J. *Jodan-uke* (upper body block)

K. *Gedan-barai* (lower body sweep)

L. *Chudan-naka-uke* (middle body block from the inside) to both sides

M. *Sage-uchi* (drop punch)

N. *Tegatana-urakake-ue-tsuki* (hand-sword back hook-upper punch)

O. *Enkei-koken-shita-uchi* (lower punch using the arc fist in a circular motion)

P. *Omote-urakake* (front-back hook)

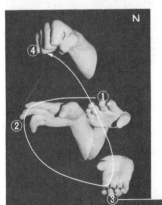

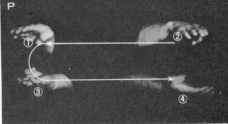

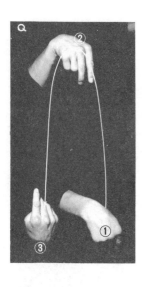

Q. *Kaiten-koken-mawashi-oroshi-uchi* (turning arc fist drop punch)

R. *Sotote-kake-oroshi-uchi* (outer hand hook drop punch)

S. *Tegatana-urakake-ue-tsuki* (hand-sword hook-upper punch)

T. *Age-uchi* (rising strike)

U. *Koken-enkei-ue-tsuki* (arc fist upper punch in a circular motion)

V. *Koken-shotei-uke* (arc fist-palm heel block)

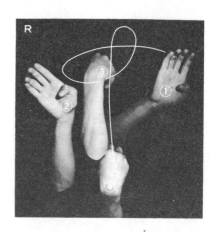

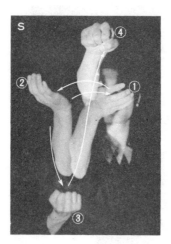

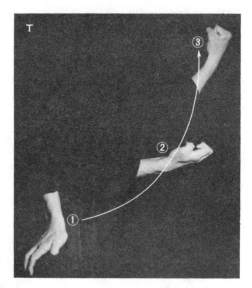

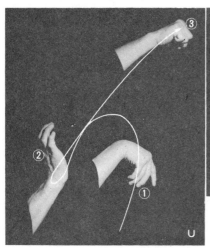

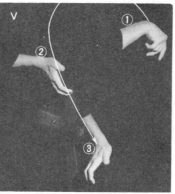

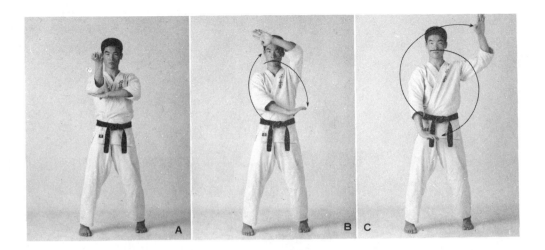

MAWASHI-UKE (ROUNDHOUSE BLOCK)

This block is one of the most important blocks in all of karate.

1. Migi-mawashi-uke (right round-house block)

A. Starting from the parallel stance, raise your right arm and bend it at the elbow. The elbow should be on a level with the chest. Next, bring the left hand across the front of the chest, turn it palm down and touch the elbow of the right arm with the wrist of the left hand.

B. The right arm is now extended downwards in a circular motion, while the left arm is being brought up with the hands crossing in front of the face.

C. The right hand is now extended straight downwards, while the left arm has continued in its circular path across the face and out to the side.

D. The hands are now in position to block punches: the right hand at shoulder level protects the upper body and face, the left hand in the hip area protects the lower body and genital area. Both defenses rely on the heels of the hands for maximum protection.

E. After the blocks have been performed, both arms are extended forward with the heels of both hands protruding in *Shotei-oshi* (palm heel thrust).

F. Side view of E.

F'. The progression of the hands into *Shotei-oshi* (palm heel thrust).

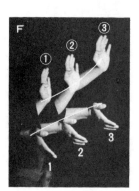

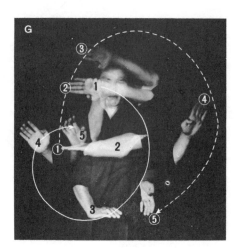

2. Hidari-mawashi-uke (left roundhouse block)

This is the same as the right roundhouse block except that it is performed in the opposite direction, as shown in G'.

ENKEI-GYAKU-TSUKI (REVERSE THRUST IN A CIRCULAR MOTION)

1. Migi-enkei-gyaku-tsuki (right reverse thrust in a circular motion)

This technique is especially useful when you are attacked from behind or from the side. When attacked in this manner, you twist your body and perform the *Tegatana-kake* (handsword hook). This technique forces you to make a 180° turn, and constant practice will sharpen your reaction time for all movements of this kind.

A. Starting in the forward stance, bring your left hand in front of the genital area in order to protect it.

B. Start moving the left arm up in the circular motion.

C. Begin to twist your body towards the left side as the arm moves back.

D. Then, block the opponent's thrust with *Tegatana-kake* (handsword hook).

E. Pulling the opponent off balance with the hook, attack with the right arm.

2. Hidari-enkei-gyaku-tsuki (left reverse thrust in a circular motion)

This is the same technique performed in the opposite direction.

A

TEGATANA-UKE (HANDSWORD BLOCK)

Of all the blocks in karate, the handsword block is the one used most often. This block should be performed in a semi-circular motion in order for it to be most successful. Again, we emphasize the fact that circular movements are essential for maximum effectiveness in karate.

1. Migi-tegatana-uke (right handsword block)

A. In the back stance, bring both hands to a position in front of the genital area.

B. Swing both hands backwards and to the left side of the body.

C. Continue following a circular path until the hands are on a level with the left ear.

B

C

D. At this point, the right hand crosses over in front of the face and starts to descend. The left hand begins to drop towards the chest.

E. The right hand is now in position to block the thrust and the left hand is guarding the vital areas of the body.

F. Follow carefully the circular patterns of the hands shown here.

D

E

F

2. Hidari-tegatana-uke (left hand-sword block)

A. This is the exact opposite of *Migi-tegatana-uke* (right handsword block). Stand in the left back stance, and bring both hands to a position in front of *Kinteki* (groin).

B. Swing both hands backwards and to the right side of the body.

C. Continue following a circular motion until the hands are on a level with the right ear.

D. At this point, the left hand crosses over in front of the face and starts to descend. The right hand begins to drop towards the chest.

E. The left hand is now in position to block the thrust and the right hand is guarding the vital areas of the body.

F. The circular movements of the hands.

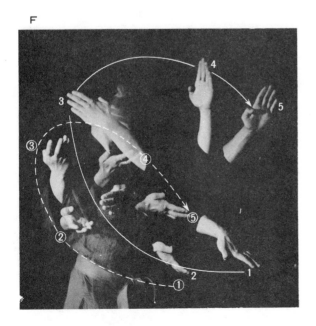

RHYTHM IN KARATE

Rhythm is defined as any kind of movement characterized by the regular recurrence of strong and weak elements. All things in the universe have rhythm, either external, like music, or internal, like the atomic structure of a rock. The martial arts are no exception, and the student who has a sense of rhythm will improve in karate much more quickly than one who does not. It would be of great assistance to a karateka to become involved in the rhythmic occurrences in everyday life such as music, dance, and so on. This will lead to a unification of the mind and body which will serve as the firm foundation for growth and excellence in any undertaking.

3. Kata

第四章
型（かた）

Kata are pre-arranged forms of demonstrating methods of attack, defense and counter-attack. In order to understand this, think of karate as a language: The basic techniques can be thought of as the letters of an alphabet; the *kata* (forms) will be the equivalent of words and sentences; the *kumite* (sparring) will be analogous to conversations.

The *kata* have been designed through hundreds of years of practice and experimentation by great masters of karate. Today, there are approximately 70 different *kata*, though only 30 of these forms are in common usage.

It is essential for the karateka to learn the *kata* totally. By this, we mean to say that you must be able to determine the correct form to use for every situation with split-second accuracy. In order to accomplish this, it is necessary to practice the *kata* from 3,000 to 10,000 times each. Remember, however, that it is better to know at least one form exceptionally well rather than 10 forms only moderately well.

TAIKYOKU 1

1. Start in the *Fudo-tachi* stance (ready stance).

2. Turn to the left and assume the *Hidari-zenkutsu-tachi* (left forward stance) while performing *Hidari-gedan-barai* (left lower body sweep).

3. Take one step forward with the right foot and perform the *Chudan-tsuki* (middle body thrust).

4. Swing the body around to the right 180° in preparation for . . .

5. . . . *Migi-gedan-barai* (right lower body sweep).

6. Perform a *Hidari-oi-tsuki* (left lunge punch).

7. Bring the left foot back next to the right. Turn and step to the left (left foot should be at a 90° angle to the right foot) and perform *Hidari-gedan-barai* (left lower body sweep).

8. Step forward with the right foot and perform *Migi-seiken-chudan-oi-tsuki* (right middle body lunge punch using the normal fist).

9. Step forward with the left foot and perform *Hidari-seiken-chudan-oi-tsuki* (left middle body lunge punch using the normal fist).

10. Step forward with the right foot and perform *Migi-seiken-chudan-oi-tsuki* (right middle body lunge punch using the normal fist).

11. Pivot 270° to the left on the right foot (the left foot should now be in front). Then, perform *Hidari-gedan-barai* (left lower body sweep).

12. Perform *Migi-chudan-oi-tsuki* (right middle body lunge punch).

13. After performing *Migi-chudan-oi-tsuki,* swing the right arm to the right and perform *Migi-gedan-barai* (right lower body sweep). This entails pivoting 180° to the right on the left foot.

14. Take one step forward and perform *Hidari-seiken-chudan-oi-tsuki* (left middle body lunge punch using the normal fist).

15. Bring the left foot back next to the right. Turn and step with the left leg 90° to the left and perform *Hidari-gedan-barai* (left lower body sweep).

16. Step forward and perform *Migi-seiken-chudan-oi-tsuki* (right middle body lunge punch using the normal fist).

17. Take one step forward and perform *Hidari-seiken-chudan-oi-tsuki* (left middle body lunge punch using the normal fist).

18. Take one step forward and perform *Migi-seiken-chudan-oi-tsuki* (right middle body lunge punch using the normal fist).

19. Turn the back leg around to the left (the whole body turns 270°), and perform *Hidari-gedan-barai* (left lower body sweep).

20. Take one step forward and perform *Migi-seiken-chudan-oi-tsuki* (right middle body lunge punch using the normal fist).

21. Turn to the right, pivoting on the left foot 180°, and perform *Migi-gedan-barai* (right lower body sweep).

22. Take one step forward and perform *Hidari-seiken-chudan-oi-tsuki* (left middle body lunge punch using the normal fist).

23. Return to the starting position.

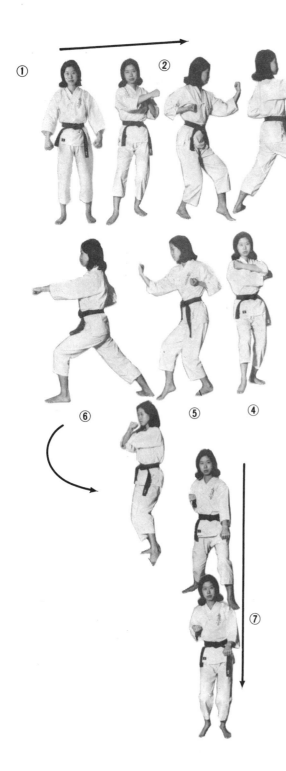

TAIKYOKU 3

1. Starting position is the same as that of the previous *kata*.

2. Turn to the left and perform the *Hidari-chudan-naka-uke* (left middle body block from inside). Here, you should be in the *Kokutsu-tachi* position (back stance). You will be in this position after each execution of *Naka-uke*.

3. Put the right foot one step forward and perform *Migi-oi-tsuki* (right lunge punch) finishing in *Zenkutsu-tachi* (forward stance). You will be in this stance following every punch.

4. Turn the right arm to the right, making a 180° turn.

5. Perform *Migi-chudan-naka-uke* (right middle body block from the inside). At this time, you should be in the *Kokutsu-tachi* position (back stance) again.

6. Put the left foot one step forward and perform *Hidari-oi-tsuki* (left lunge punch).

7. Turn the left leg 90° to the left, stepping into *Zenkutsu-tachi* (forward stance) and perform *Hidari-gedan-barai* (left lower body sweep).

8. Take one step forward and perform *Migi-jodan-oi-tsuki* (right upper body lunge punch).

9. Take one step forward and perform *Hidari-jodan-oi-tsuki* (left upper body lunge punch).

10. Then step forward and perform *Migi-jodan-oi-tsuki* (right upper body lunge punch).

11. Using the right foot as a pivoting foot, turn 270° to the left and perform *Hidari-chudan-naka-uke* (left middle body block from the inside).

12. Take one step forward and perform *Migi-chudan-oi-tsuki* (right middle body lunge punch).

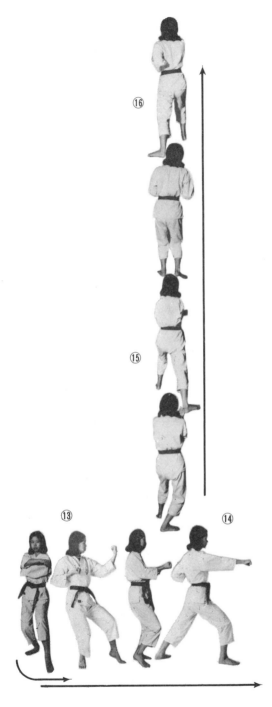

13. Make a 180° turn to the right and perform *Migi-chudan-naka-uke* (right middle body block from the inside).

14. Take one step forward and perform *Hidari-chudan-tsuki* (left middle body thrust).

NOTE: The photographs for steps 13 and 14 show the karateka with her hands and feet in the wrong positions.

15. Make a 90° turn to the left and perform *Hidari-gedan-barai* (left lower body sweep). You should be in *Zenkutsu-tachi* position (forward stance) at this moment.

16. Step forward and perform *Migi-jodan-tsuki* (right upper body thrust).

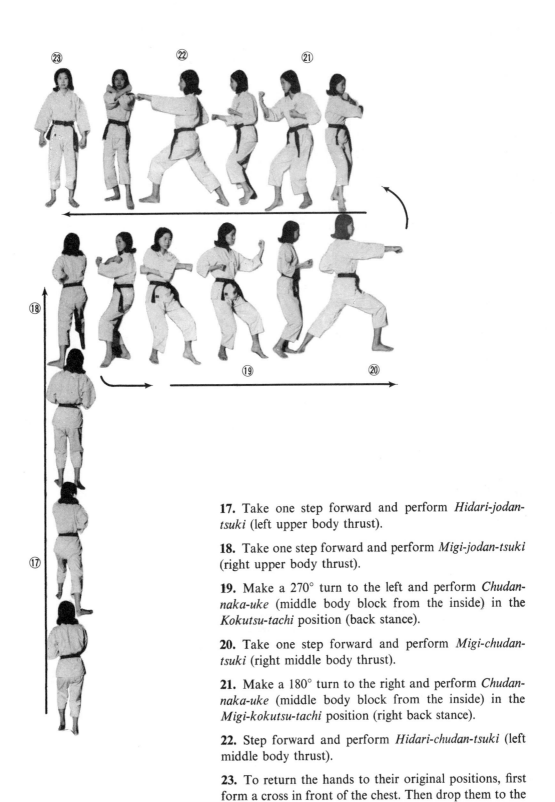

17. Take one step forward and perform *Hidari-jodan-tsuki* (left upper body thrust).

18. Take one step forward and perform *Migi-jodan-tsuki* (right upper body thrust).

19. Make a 270° turn to the left and perform *Chudan-naka-uke* (middle body block from the inside) in the *Kokutsu-tachi* position (back stance).

20. Take one step forward and perform *Migi-chudan-tsuki* (right middle body thrust).

21. Make a 180° turn to the right and perform *Chudan-naka-uke* (middle body block from the inside) in the *Migi-kokutsu-tachi* position (right back stance).

22. Step forward and perform *Hidari-chudan-tsuki* (left middle body thrust).

23. To return the hands to their original positions, first form a cross in front of the chest. Then drop them to the starting position.

HEIAN 4

1. Start by taking the *Fudo-tachi* stance (ready stance).

2. Place the left foot one step to the left while reaching across the body with the left hand and placing it on top of the right one.

3. The left hand now performs *Chudan-tegatana-uke* (middle body handsword block), and the right hand performs *Jodan-tegatana-uke* (upper body handsword block).

4. Bring both hands to the left side of the body with the right hand above the left one while bringing the left foot back towards the right.

5. Place the right foot one step to the right. The right hand performs *Chudan-tegatana-uke* (middle body handsword block) and the left hand performs *Jodan-tegatana-uke* (upper body handsword block). You should now be in the *Kokutsu-tachi* stance (back stance).

6. Take one step forward with the left foot and perform *Gedan-juji-uke* (lower body X-block).

7. Take one step forward with the right foot and perform *Morote-naka-uke* (two-hand block from the inside).

8. Bring the back foot forward and place it next to the front foot. Bring both hands to the right side of the body.

9. Attack the opponent with *Hidari-ashigatana* (left footsword) and *Hidari-uraken* (left back fist) at the same time.

10. As you bring the left foot down, assume the *Zenkutsu-tachi* position (forward stance). The right elbow comes across to the left hand to perform *Hiji-uchi* (elbow thrust). Keep the right hand in *Tettsui* position (iron hammer fist).

11. Bring both feet together; place the right hand above the left one at the left side of the body.

12. Perform *Migi-yoko-geri* (right side kick) and *Migi-uraken* (right back fist).

13. As you bring the right foot down, bring the left elbow across to the right hand using *Hiji-uchi* (elbow thrust). Keep the left hand in *Tettsui* (iron hammer fist).

14. Twist the body around to the left until you are facing forward. The left arm should be stretched out to the front slightly above eye level. The right hand should be on a level with the ear. Continue twisting the body to the left and assume a left forward stance (*Hidari-zenkutsu-tachi*). At this point, the position of the hands should be reversed.

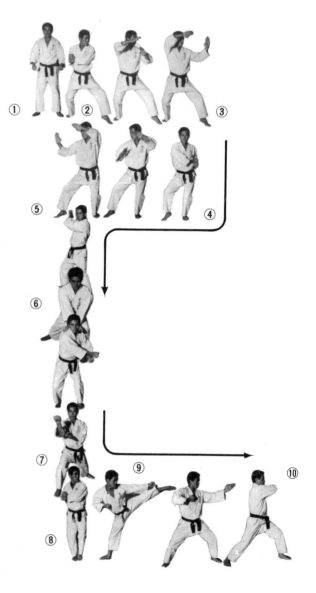

15. Now perform a *Migi-mae-geri* (right front kick).

16. Jump one step to the side and assume *Kake-ashi-tachi* (hooked foot stance), then attack the opponent's face using *Migi-uraken* (right back fist).

17. Place the right foot towards the right side at a 45° angle from the left foot. Cross both hands in front of the chest.

18. Uncross the hands . . .

19. . . . and perform *Migi-mae-geri* (right front kick).

20. As you bring your foot down, step forward and perform *Hidari-seiken-chudan-tsuki* (left middle body thrust with normal fist).

21. Perform *Migi-chudan-tsuki* (right middle body thrust). It is of particular importance that 20 and 21 be performed in rapid succession.

22. Step around with the right foot and bring the right hand to the back at a 45° angle from the middle of the right side and cross both hands in front of the chest.

23. As you uncross the hands . . .

24. . . . perform *Hidari-mae-geri* (left front kick).

25. Bring the left foot down, assume *Zenkutsu-tachi* (forward stance), and perform *Migi-chudan-tsuki* (right middle body thrust).

26. Then, perform *Hidari-chudan-tsuki* (left middle body thrust). It is of particular importance that the right and left hand movements be performed in rapid succession.

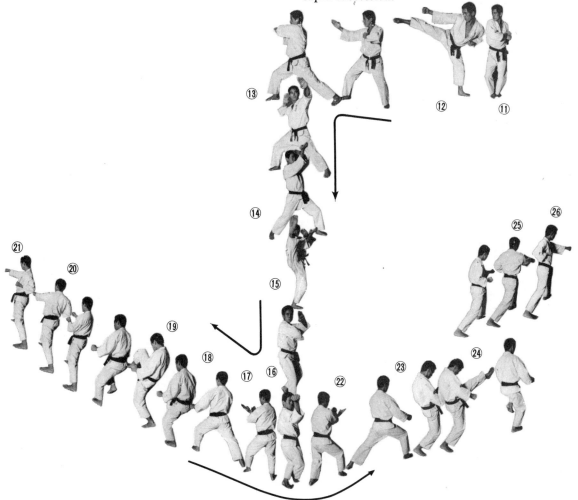

27. As you bring the left foot to the center-line . . .

28. . . . perform *Hidari-chudan-morote-naka-uke* (left middle body two-hand block from the inside).

29. Then, stepping forward with the right foot, perform *Migi-chudan-morote-naka-uke* (right middle body two-hand block from the inside).

30. Step forward with the left foot and perform *Hidari-chudan-morote-naka-uke* (left two-hand middle body block from the inside).

31. Remaining in the same position, raise both hands and attack the opponent by grabbing his hair or neck.

32. Pull down the opponent's head by grabbing his hair, and attack him with *Migi-hiza-geri* (right knee kick).

33. As you bring the right foot down, turn to the left.

34. Perform *Hidari-tegatana-uke* (left handsword block).

35. Take one step forward with the right foot and perform *Migi-tegatana-uke* (right handsword block).

36. Return to the original position.

HEIAN 5

1. Assume the ready stance.

2. Put the left foot one step to the left and assume *Kokutsu-tachi* position (back stance). Bring the left arm to the right side of the body and the right arm to the left side of the body.

3. Remaining in the *Kokutsu-tachi* position, perform *Chudan-naka-uke* with the left hand (middle body block from the inside). At the same time, withdraw the right hand.

4. Perform *Chudan-gyaku-tsuki* (middle body thrust from the reverse position).

5. Bring the right foot close to the left foot, and at the same time, place the left hand on top of the right hand at the right side of the body.

6. Place the right foot one step to the right and bring the right hand towards the left underarm.

7. Assume *Kokutsu-tachi* (back stance) and perform *Migi-chudan-naka-uke* (right middle body block from the inside).

8. Remaining in the same position, perform *Hidari-chudan-tsuki* (left middle body thrust).

9. Bring the left foot next to the right foot and put both hands together at the left side of the body.

10. Take one step forward with the right foot and assume *Zenkutsu-tachi* position (forward stance) while performing *Migi-chudan-morote-naka-uke* (right middle body two-hand block from the inside).

11. Take one step forward with the left foot bringing both hands up to the right side of the head and perform *Gedan-juji-uke* (lower body X-block).

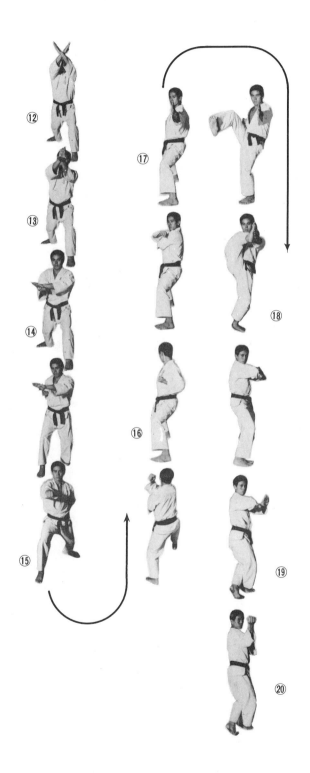

12. Then, quickly, raise both hands and perform *Juji-ue-uke* (X-block from below).

13. Gradually lower the hands, and at the same time rotate the left wrist until the left palm is facing up.

14. The hands should be on a level with the chest at the right side of the body with the wrists touching.

15. Take one step forward with the right foot and perform *Migi-chudan-tsuki* (right middle body thrust).

16. Turn the right leg around to the back and assume *Kiba-tachi* position (horse stance), and perform *Gedan-barai* (lower body sweep).

17. Remaining in *Kiba-tachi* (horse stance), cross the arms in front of the chest, and then stretch out the right arm to the right and the left arm to the left.

18. Touch the palm of the left hand with the *Soko-ashi* (arch of the foot) of the right foot, then quickly assume *Kiba-tachi* (horse stance) again.

19. As you take the *Kake-ashi-tachi* position (hooked foot stance), get ready to strike an opponent with the *Migi-uraken* (right back fist).

20. Attack the opponent with *Migi-uraken* (right back fist) and *Hidari-shotei* (left palm heel thrust).

21. Place the left leg one step to the left side and raise the right arm.

22. Jump into the air and shout a forceful, *Kiai!* (*Kiai* is the traditional Japanese term shouted when performing an attack). While in the air, bend both legs at the knee and perform *Gedan-juji-uke* (lower body X-block) with both hands.

23. As you land, assume the *Zenkutsu-tachi* (forward stance) with the right leg in front. Then perform *Migi-naka-uke* (right hand block from the inside).

24. Drop the back leg (left leg) farther to the back in order to widen the stance. Cross the left arm in front of the chest so that the left hand is beside the right ear. The right arm crosses beneath the left arm and the right hand shields the lower body. Bend the left knee to lower the stance. The right hand may be used to grab an opponent by the ankle in order to trip him.

25. The right arm is raised to the side. The karateka is now in a horse stance and performing *Gedan-barai* (lower body sweep) with the left hand.

26. Bring the right foot over to the left one so that both heels are touching.

27. Then, step forward with the right foot at a 45° angle assuming the *Kiba-tachi* (horse stance). Cross the right arm in front of the chest so that the right hand is beside the left ear. The left arm crosses beneath the right arm and the left hand protects the lower body.

28. Bend the right knee to lower the stance. The left hand is used to grab an opponent by the ankle in order to trip him. Reassume the *Kiba-tachi* and perform *Gedan-barai* (lower body sweep) with the right hand. The left arm is raised to the side.

29. Bring the right leg back to the original position and assume the *Fudo-tachi* (ready stance).

㉓ ㉔ ㉕ ㉖ ㉗ ㉘ ㉙

SAIHA

1. Assume ready stance.

2. Assume the *Musubi-tachi* (linked foot stance) and meditate.

3. Cross the arms in front of the chest so that the right hand is beside the left ear and the left hand is beside the the right ear. Gradually open the arms and assume the *Fudo-tachi* (ready stance).

4. Place the right foot diagonally one step forward making a 45° angle with the body.

5. Bring the left foot over to the right foot and assume the *Musubi-tachi* (linked foot stance). At the same time, bring the right hand up to the armpit and place the left hand over it.

6. Attack the opponent's jaw with the right elbow.

7. Place the left foot one step to the side and assume the *Han-kiba-tachi* (half horse stance). Attack the opponent's face using *Uraken* (back fist) and at the same time shield the solar plexus with the left hand using the *Shotei* (palm heel).

8. Place the left foot diagonally one step forward to make a 45° angle with the body.